A dream had come true! Your friend had managed to get seats near the dugout for the third game of the 1989 World Series in San Francisco, California. You were excited as you settled into your seat. You had never been this close to the action before. The umpire was sweeping off home plate. The game was about to begin and suddenly you felt your seat wiggle and shake. In fact, everything began to shake! What was happening?

San Andreas Fault

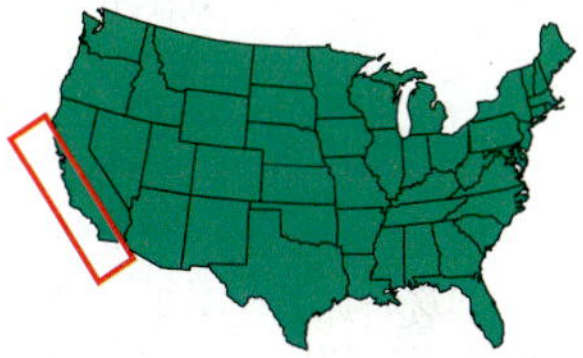

The aerial photograph on this page is of the Carrizo Plain. It shows a part of the San Andreas fault. The fault is a group of fractures, or cracks, in the earth's rocky surface where earthquake movements have taken place. It runs roughly parallel to the coastline of California. In some places, the fault can be seen at the earth's surface. In other places, it lies beneath the surface or is under water.

A fault is also a line where rock on one side of the fault might move up, down, or sideways in relation to rock on the other side. An earthquake is a sudden, rapid shaking of a part of the earth's crust caused by the release of energy stored underground in rocks. On October 17, 1989, movement along the San Andreas fault caused one of the strongest earthquakes along the fault in recent history. The earthquake began in the Santa Cruz Mountains near Loma Prieta Peak. Yet, people as far away as the states of Oregon and Nevada felt the shaking.

- What does the inside of the earth look like?
- How old is the earth?
- What causes earthquakes?

Unit E

EARTH MOVEMENTS

Chapter 1

Chapter 2

Chapter 3

Using a map to help locate the fault

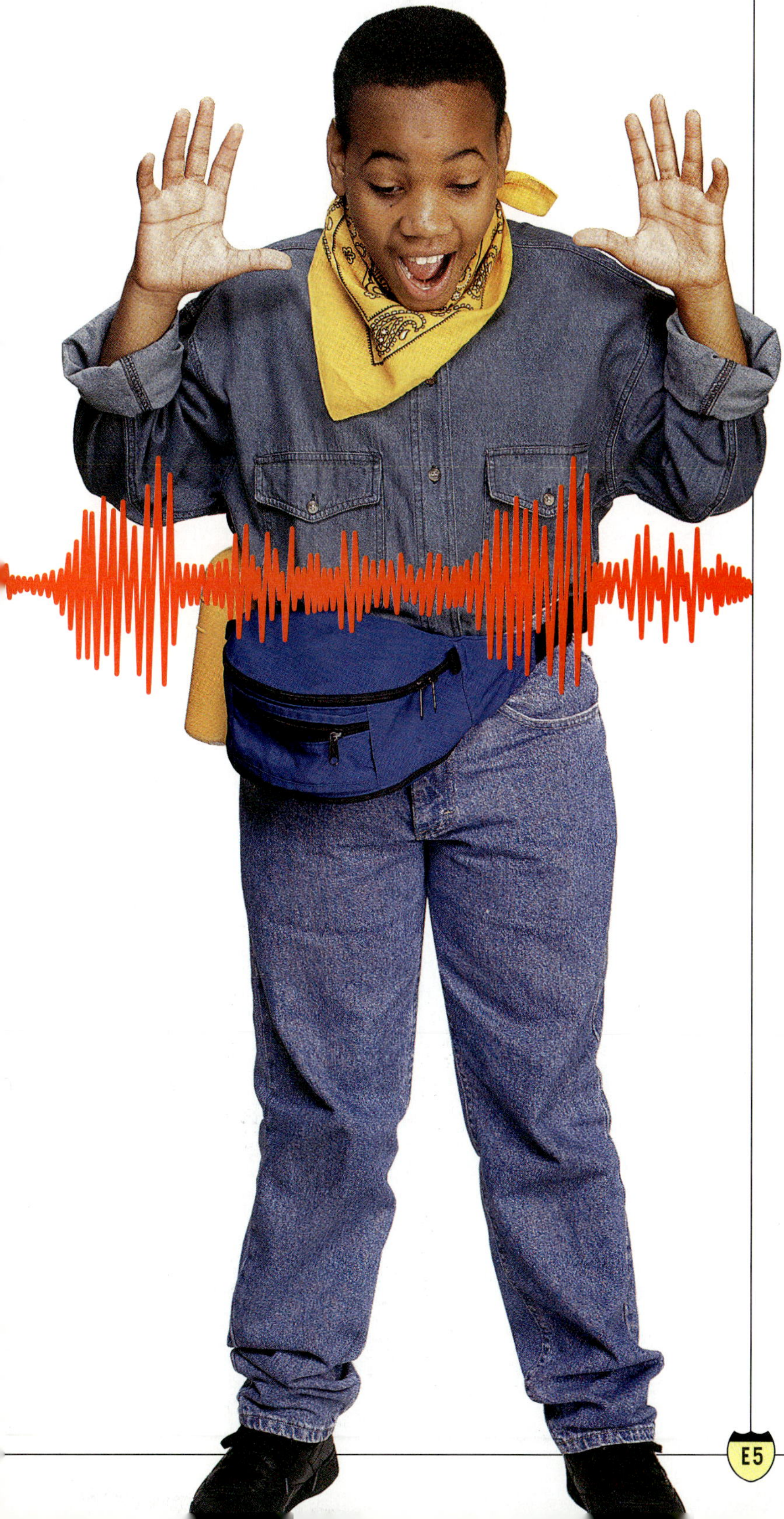

Activities

Features

Chapter 1

The Earth's Layers

A broken fence showing displacement along the San Andreas fault.

▲ Damage caused by the 1906 San Francisco earthquake. Note the twisted tram tracks, cracks in the street, and buckled sidewalks.

Much of the movement along the San Andreas fault is horizontal. This horizontal movement occurs when great blocks of rock move sideways slowly past each other. Land on the western side of the fault moves toward the northwest. Land on the eastern side of the fault moves toward the southeast.

Railroad tracks, roads, fences, or anything that crosses the fault can be broken or offset when movement occurs. Even stream beds may turn sharply where they cross the fault. In fact, movement along the fault in 1857 offset some stream channels by almost 10 meters.

The students in the photograph are standing along the San Andreas fault. Imagine that you are with them. What might you see if you looked down at the fault? You might expect to see a single fracture or crack in the ground. However, the San Andreas fault is a system of many fractures about 1,200 kilometers long and as much as 16 kilometers deep.

Now imagine that you could go down into the earth to investigate the San Andreas fault. What kinds of rocks do you think you would see? What would you see if you could continue your journey toward the center of the earth? What do you think the earth's interior would look like? How would the temperature change as you plunged toward the center of our planet?

SCIENCE JOURNAL

The earth has three layers. Rocks and soils make up most of the crust, or outer layer. Look around your home and neighborhood. In your Science Journal, list ways that people use rocks and soils.

Explore Activity

How are the earth's layers studied?

Process Skills
Making models, Inferring, Communicating

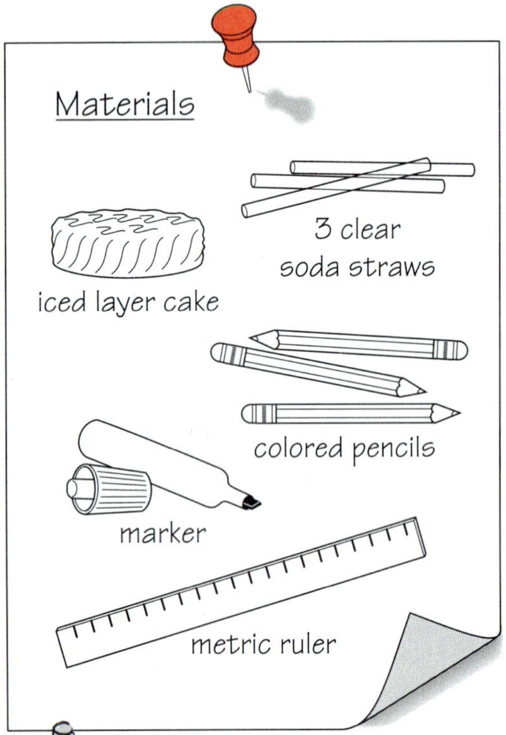

Observe and Collect Data

1. Observe the cake. In your Activity Journal, write down as many properties about the cake as you can. Some properties you will be able to see, such as the color of the icing. Other properties, such as the flavor of the cake or the number of layers, you will have to infer, or guess, based on your observations.
2. Now, gently push one straw straight into the top of the cake. Do not tilt the straw. Push the straw until it reaches the bottom of the cake.
3. Carefully remove the straw from the cake. Label the straw "A" with the marker.
4. Repeat steps 2 and 3 with the two remaining straws in different parts of the cake. Make certain that the samples are taken along a straight line. Label the straws "B" and "C."
5. Place the three straws in order in front of you. Use the ruler and colored pencils to draw a cross section of the cake from what you see in the straws. A cross section is a cutaway, or side, view of an area. In this case, it is a sketch of what the cake would look like if you cut it in half and viewed it along the cut.

Share Your Results

How is your cross section like other students' cross sections? How is it different?

Draw Conclusions

1. Which of your inferences about the cake were like your observations?
2. Which inferences were different from your observations?
3. How did the straws allow you to "see" inside the cake?

Apply What you Know

1. Scientists who study the earth's soil use a similar method to take soil samples. Their instruments are much like your straws, but the instruments are made of a different material. What do you think this material is? Explain your answer.
2. Would it be possible to use this method to sample rocks deep within the earth? Explain your answer.

How did the earth's layers form and what are they like?

Our planet might have formed in stages.

▲ Early in its formation, the earth was a vast collection of unsorted particles.

▲ As it heated and cooled, denser elements moved toward the earth's center.

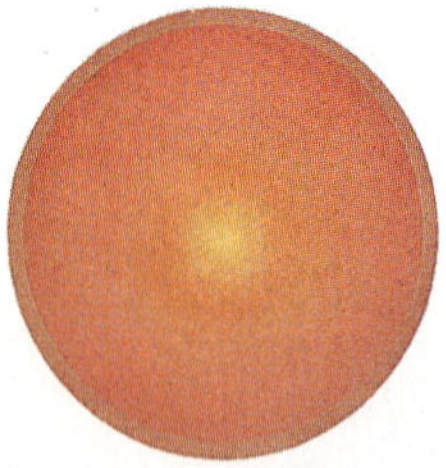

▲ Lighter elements moved toward the earth's surface to form its crust.

If you could cut the earth in half, you would see that it is made of layers. The outermost layer is the **crust.** The innermost layer is the **core**. The **mantle** (man´təl) lies between the crust and the core. How do you think these layers might have formed?

Most scientists think that the earth, and the other planets, formed from a huge, hot ball of gases, dust, and other elements. As the ball heated and cooled over millions and millions of years, the densest elements sank to the earth's center. Other elements accumulated to form the middle layer. The lightest elements rose and became the earth's outermost layer. Many of the gases combined to form the oceans and atmosphere.

The earth's rocky crust is its thinnest layer. There are two types of crust: continental crust and oceanic crust. Continental crust forms the earth's landmasses. Mountains and valleys are made of continental crust. The highest point on the earth's crust is Mount Everest in Asia. It is nearly 9 kilometers high.

Oceanic crust is found below the earth's oceans. The deepest point on the earth is found in the Pacific Ocean. It is the Mariana Trench, and it reaches to a depth of more than 11 kilometers below sea level.

Below the crust is the mantle, the thickest layer of the earth. The mantle has two parts. The upper 100 kilometers of this middle layer are rigid, or stiff. Below this rigid part, the mantle is partly melted. Sometimes this partly melted material behaves like a brittle solid. Sometimes it behaves like soft putty.

Crust
The crust is the thinnest layer of the earth. Continental crust is about 35 kilometers thick. Oceanic crust is about 8 kilometers thick.

Outer Core
The earth's core has two parts. The hot, liquid, outer core is about 2,270 kilometers thick.

Inner Core
The earth's solid inner core is about 1,210 kilometers in radius.

Mantle
The earth's mantle is about 2,900 kilometers thick. The mantle is a hot layer of rocks. Temperatures in this layer might be as high as 4,000°C and the rocks can bend like red-hot metal.

The core is the innermost layer of the earth. This hot, dense sphere has two parts. The outer core is liquid. A recent hypothesis suggests that the outer core has ridges, peaks, and valleys several kilometers deep and high over its surface. This liquid outer core surrounds a solid inner core.

Be a Scientist

HANDS-ON ACTIVITY

How is an egg like the earth?

1. Carefully cut a hard-boiled egg in half with its shell on. On one half, put a small dot in the center of the yolk with a permanent marker.
2. ACTIVITY JOURNAL Study the flat side of the egg. Make a sketch of it in your Activity Journal. To one side of the sketch, label the shell, egg white, yolk, and dot.
3. On the other side of the drawing, label the parts of the egg that could represent different layers of the earth. How accurate do you think your model is? What could you do to make it more accurate?

How do scientists know about the earth's interior?

Scientists have drilled nearly 12 kilometers into the earth's crust. In the drawing of the earth shown on page E11, you can see that the earth's diameter is almost 12,800 kilometers. How do you think scientists find out about the rest of the earth?

Much of what we now know about the earth's interior comes from studying meteorites. A meteorite is a chunk of rock that traveled through our solar system and fell to the earth's surface. Some meteorites are made mostly of iron. Which layer of the earth is mostly iron? Some meteorites are made of materials much like peridotite. Which layer of the earth is mostly peridotite?

Scientists believe that meteorites formed at the same time as our planet. They also think that the planets and meteorites formed from the same cloud of dust and gases. Thus, by studying meteorites, scientists can hypothesize about the composition of the earth's interior.

What evidence do scientists have that the earth is divided into three layers? The division of the earth into the crust, the mantle, and the core is based on studies of earthquake waves.

Most earthquakes occur along faults, such as the San Andreas fault. Waves of energy are caused by a sudden movement along a fault. These earthquake waves move through the earth in all directions. The waves behave differently when they travel through different materials. By studying the ways these waves travel through the earth, scientists are able to identify three major boundaries in the earth's interior.

▲ The earth's middle layer, the mantle, is possibly made of a rock called peridotite. Peridotite contains minerals rich in iron and magnesium. Earthquake waves travel faster through the mantle than they do through the earth's crust.

▲ The earth's core is a very hot, dense sphere probably made of iron and nickel. Iron and nickel are very heavy elements. Some earthquake waves travel only through solids. How do you think scientists found out that the outer core is liquid?

DILEMMA

Deep Drilling

Scientists are planning to drill deep into the earth along the San Andreas fault. The information they find may help us to better understand our planet. Perhaps the data will provide clues to some of the other planets in our solar system. Drilling these holes, however, could create huge amounts of waste rock materials.

SCIENCE JOURNAL

Think About It Should the holes be drilled? Why or why not? What should be done with the waste? Write your opinion in your Science Journal and explain your reasons.

▲ There are two kinds of crust. Continental crust, which makes up the earth's landmasses, is made mostly of granite. Granite is a rock rich in elements such as silicon, potassium, aluminum, and magnesium. Oceanic crust makes up the ocean floors. Oceanic crust is mostly basalt. Basalt is rich in silicon, calcium, aluminum, iron, and magnesium.

How are you doing?

1. From the center of the earth outward, what are the layers of the earth? Which is the thinnest? The thickest?
2. Describe the earth's mantle.
3. **Think** Which fruit, an apple or a peach, is a better model of the earth? Explain why.
4. **Think** Which kind of crust—continental or oceanic—is more dense? Explain.

What are mountains?

Have you ever been mountain climbing? A mountain can be any feature that is higher than the surrounding land. It can be a very high hill. So if you've climbed a hill, you've been mountain climbing!

Whether you've climbed a hill or the peaks of the Rockies, the part of the mountain you saw above the earth's surface is only a small part of that mountain. Sometimes mountains are compared to icebergs. Have you ever heard the expression, "It's just the tip of the iceberg"?

An iceberg is a huge chunk of ice that has broken off a glacier. Nearly 90 percent of an iceberg is below water.

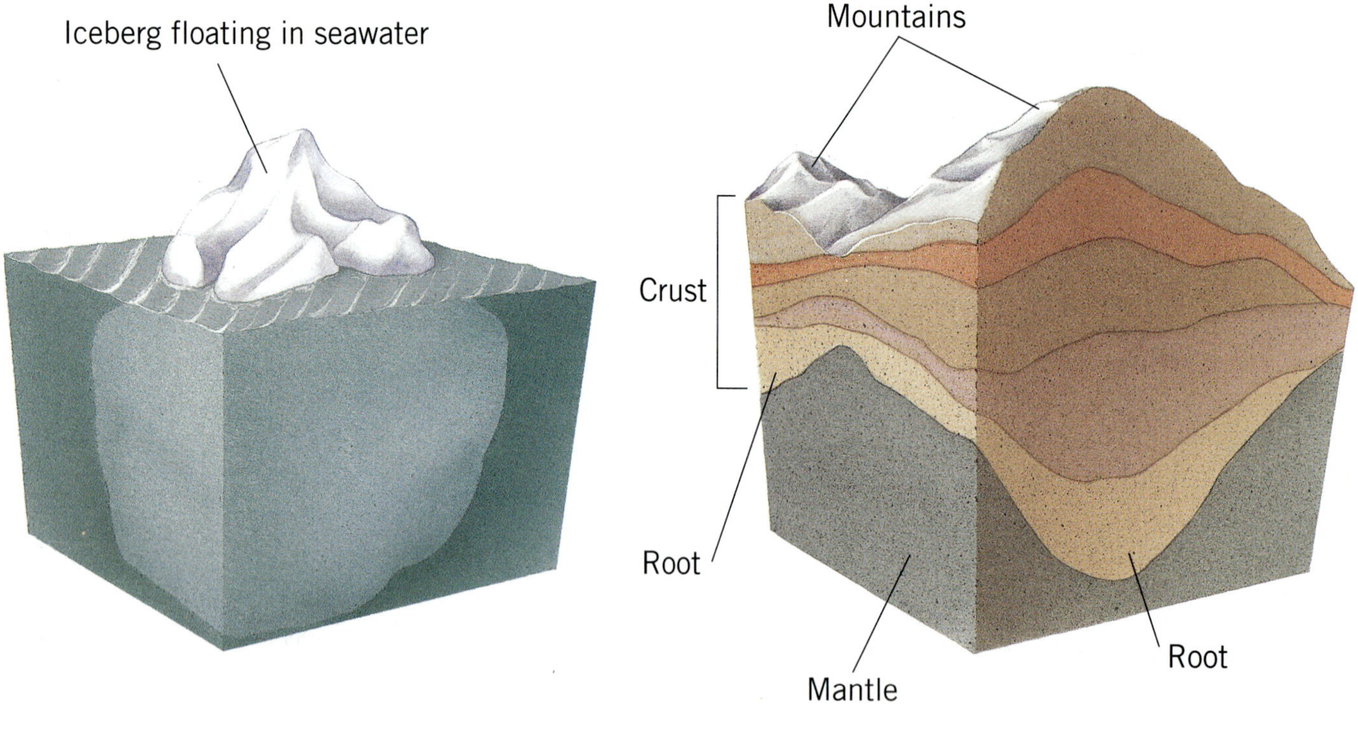

Be a Scientist

How can a mountain sink?

1. Carefully cut off the top 8 centimeters of a 2-liter plastic bottle. Then fill the bottle with water to about 2–3 centimeters from the top.
2. Fill a baby-food jar half-full with water. Put the lid on the jar. **Predict** how much of the jar will be above the water level when you place it into the bottle. Use masking tape to mark the predicted level "A."
3. ACTIVITY JOURNAL Place the baby-food jar into the water. Note the water level on the outside of the jar. Use labels to mark this water level "B." How did your prediction, "A," match your observation, "B"? In your Activity Journal, use your results to estimate how much of your "mountain"—the baby-food jar—was below the earth's surface.

If these pieces of ice are so big, why do they float? Icebergs float because they displace, or push away, a certain volume of the sea water in which they are floating.

Recall that the earth's continental crust is made mostly of granite. The mantle is made of peridotite, a much denser rock. Just as an iceberg floats in water, the lighter crust "floats" on the denser mantle. The same volume of the earth's crust weighs less than the same volume of mantle. In fact, mountains are said to have vast "roots" that support them. The roots of a mountain are the thickest part of the mountain that sinks into the mantle. If a mountain's surface erodes away, the mountain weighs less and rises. The root also rises.

◀ Just as icebergs float in water, mountains on the earth "float" on the mantle below. The higher the mountain is, the deeper the root.

How do mountains form?

There are three major mountain systems in the world. One system is along the west coast of North and South America. Another system crosses Europe and Asia. The third system is the peaks of land in the Pacific Ocean, in east Asia, and Australia.

Mountains form as the result of many processes within the earth's crust and upper mantle. Geologists have identified several major processes of mountain building. These include folding, faulting, uplift, and volcanism. Folding produces mountains marked by

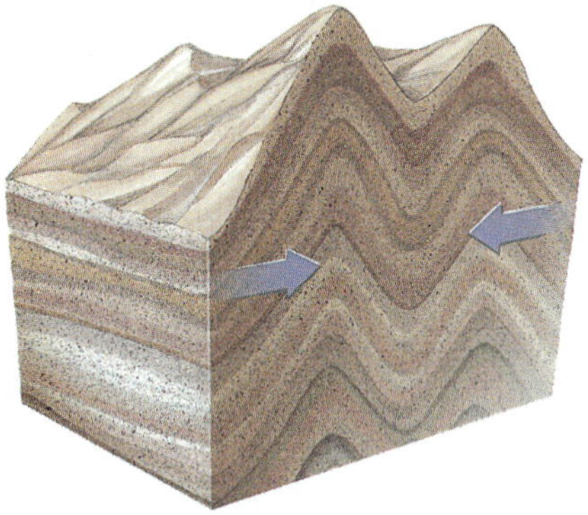

Fold mountains
When sections of the crust and upper mantle are squeezed from opposite sides, the crust wrinkles and fold mountains are formed. The Appalachians are fold mountains.

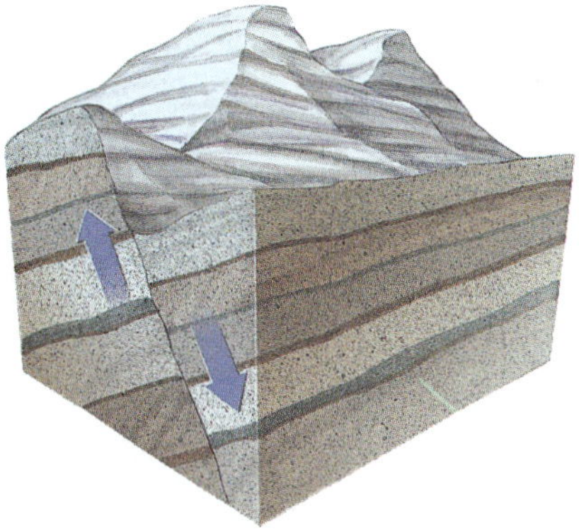

Block mountains
Block mountains have a fault along at least one side. These kinds of mountains have a steep side and a sloping side. The Teton Range in Wyoming are block mountains.

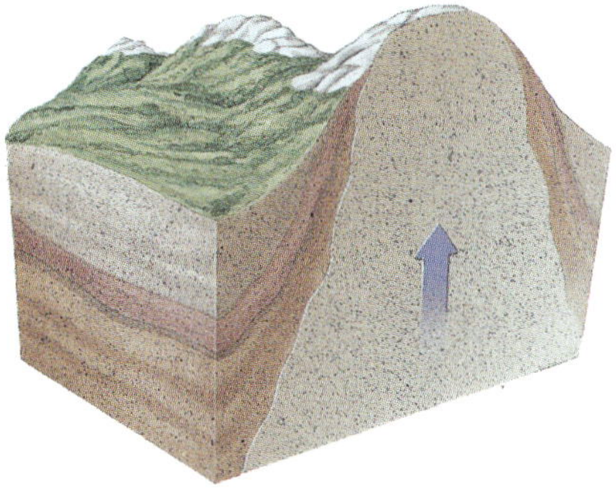

Dome mountains
Dome mountains form when large portions of the earth's crust are pushed upward by magma. The Black Hills in South Dakota are dome mountains, which are igneous rock.

valleys and parallel ridges. Faulting of large blocks of rock results in sharply rising block mountains. Uplifting results in dome mountains. What kind of mountains do you think are the result of volcanic activity?

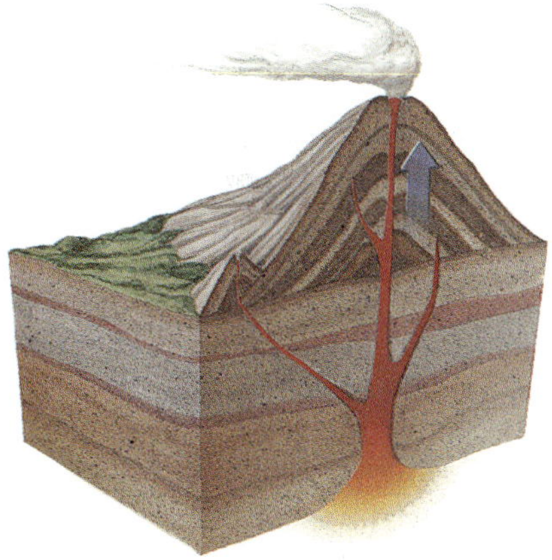

Volcanoes

Volcanoes are cone-shaped mountains that form when melted rock material piles up and hardens. Note how Mount Hood, a volcano in Oregon, is cone-shaped.

Be a Scientist

Can you model mountain building?

1. Use a plastic knife and three balls of clay. Flatten each ball into a slab about 1 centimeter thick.
2. Stack the clay slabs, separating the layers with plastic wrap. Use the clay to form fold mountains, then dome mountains, and, finally, block mountains.
3. 

In your Activity Journal, record the way you formed each mountain type. Also include a sketch of each model and label it.

How are you doing?

1. How are mountains like icebergs?
2. How do fold mountains form?
3. **Think** Compare and contrast block, dome, and volcanic mountains.
4. **Think** The San Andreas is a fault, but along most parts of the fault, it does not form block mountains. Explain why.

Looking Back

MINDS-ON ASSESSMENT

Words and Concepts

Use the correct word or phrase to complete the statement.

1. The _______ is the thinnest layer of the earth.
   a. inner core **c.** mantle
   b. outer core **d.** crust
2. Temperatures in the earth's _______ may be as high as 4,000°C.
   a. inner core **c.** mantle
   b. outer core **d.** crust
3. The earth's inner core is made mostly of _______.
   a. granite **c.** meteorites
   b. iron **d.** peridotite
4. The San Andreas fault is a feature of the earth's _______.
   a. crust **c.** inner core
   b. mantle **d.** outer core
5. _______ form when melted rock builds up and hardens to form mountains.
   a. Block mountains **c.** Fold mountains
   b. Volcanoes **d.** Dome mountains
6. When sections of the earth's crust and upper mantle are squeezed from opposite sides, _______ mountains are formed.
   a. block **c.** volcanic
   b. fold **d.** dome

Applied Thinking Skills

Answer the following questions. You can use words, drawings, and diagrams in your answers.

7. Which do you think is denser—the earth's inner core or the outer core? Explain.
8. Draw a model of Mount McKinley, an Alaskan mountain that towers about 6,200 meters above the earth's surface. Be sure to show the percentage of rock above and below the earth's surface.
9. What do volcanoes tell us about the earth's interior?
10. **Your World** Are there any faults in your state? Find out. Then explain why earthquakes could occur along any fault.

Show What You Know

Can you model the earth?

Observe and Collect Data

1. In this chapter, find the thickness of each layer of the earth. Record these values in a data table in your Activity Journal.
2. Decide on a scale to use for your model of the earth. For example, the diameter of the earth is about 12,800 kilometers. You might choose a scale of 3 centimeters = 1,000 kilometers. At this scale, the diameter of your model would be 38.4 centimeters.
3. Now, draw a cross section of the earth on the sheet of butcher paper. Draw the layers so they are the proper thickness for a model this size. Use different colors for different layers.
4. Label your model with the layer's name, thickness, and scale used. In your Activity Journal, write a brief description of each layer of the earth.

Draw Conclusions

1. Compare your model with other students' models. How are they the same?
2. How does your model differ from other students' models?
3. How accurate is your model?

Process Skills
Measuring, Communicating, Making models

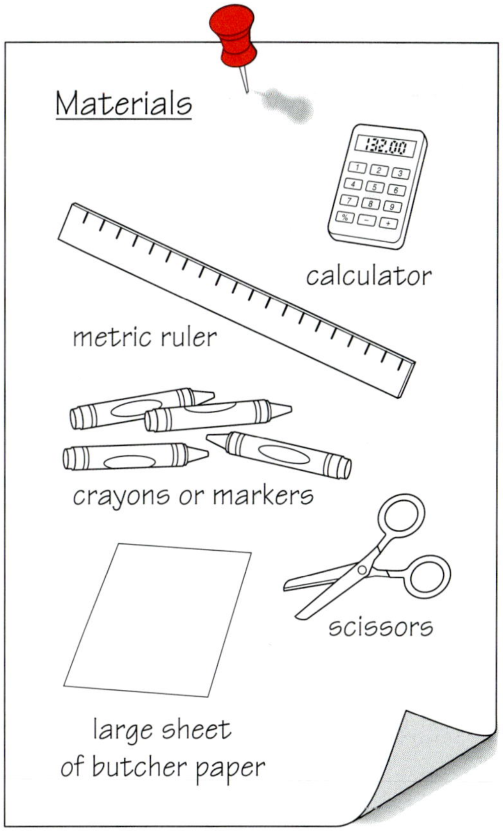

Chapter 2

The Earth's History

What kind of creature do you think the students are observing? Does the animal remind you of any other kind of animal?

Some lizards look somewhat like animals that once roamed the earth. Can you guess which ones? If you said dinosaurs, you're right! Dinosaurs lived on our planet millions of years ago. Some were huge and might have been more than 40 meters long. Others were quite small—much like the lizard shown in the photograph. Some dinosaurs were meat eaters and some ate plants. Most lived on land while others spent some of their time in water.

Dinosaurs disappeared from our planet about 65 million years ago along with some marine creatures. What may have caused these creatures to become **extinct** (ek stiŋkt´)? Might the earth's climate have changed too quickly for them to adapt? Might erupting volcanoes or earthquakes have caused their extinction? Could a meteorite have collided with the earth and caused these creatures to die?

SCIENCE JOURNAL

Imagine that you were a dinosaur that roamed the earth millions of years ago. Where did you live? How did you move from place to place? What did you eat? What did your neighbors look like? Remember, they were probably other dinosaurs—people didn't exist yet. Write your ideas in your Science Journal. Include a self-portrait.

Sometimes Western fence lizards are called blue-belly lizards.

This whale vertebra fossil was found in a sandstone layer of an ancient seabed.

Explore Activity

How do scientists find out about ancient animals?

Process Skills
Inferring, Communicating, Hypothesizing

Observe and Collect Data

1. Study the fossil shown in the photograph.
2. ACTIVITY JOURNAL In your Activity Journal, draw a possible shape and possible body covering of the animal. Include as many features as you can infer from the fossil.
3. Describe the animal. **Predict** how you think it moved, what it ate, where it lived, and so on.

Share Your Results

Compare your drawing with those of several other students. How are the drawings the same? What reasoning did all of you use to draw similar conclusions about the animal?

Draw Conclusions

1. Now your teacher will show you how scientists think the animal looked. How is your drawing similar or different?
2. What can you tell from an animal's skeleton?

Apply What You Know

Imagine that scientists found some ancient animal's bones and teeth. From this evidence, do you think that the scientist might be able to tell what kinds of plants and animals once lived on the earth? Or what the earth's climate was like? What might they do or what information might they use to help them put the bones and teeth together? What was the earth like in the past?

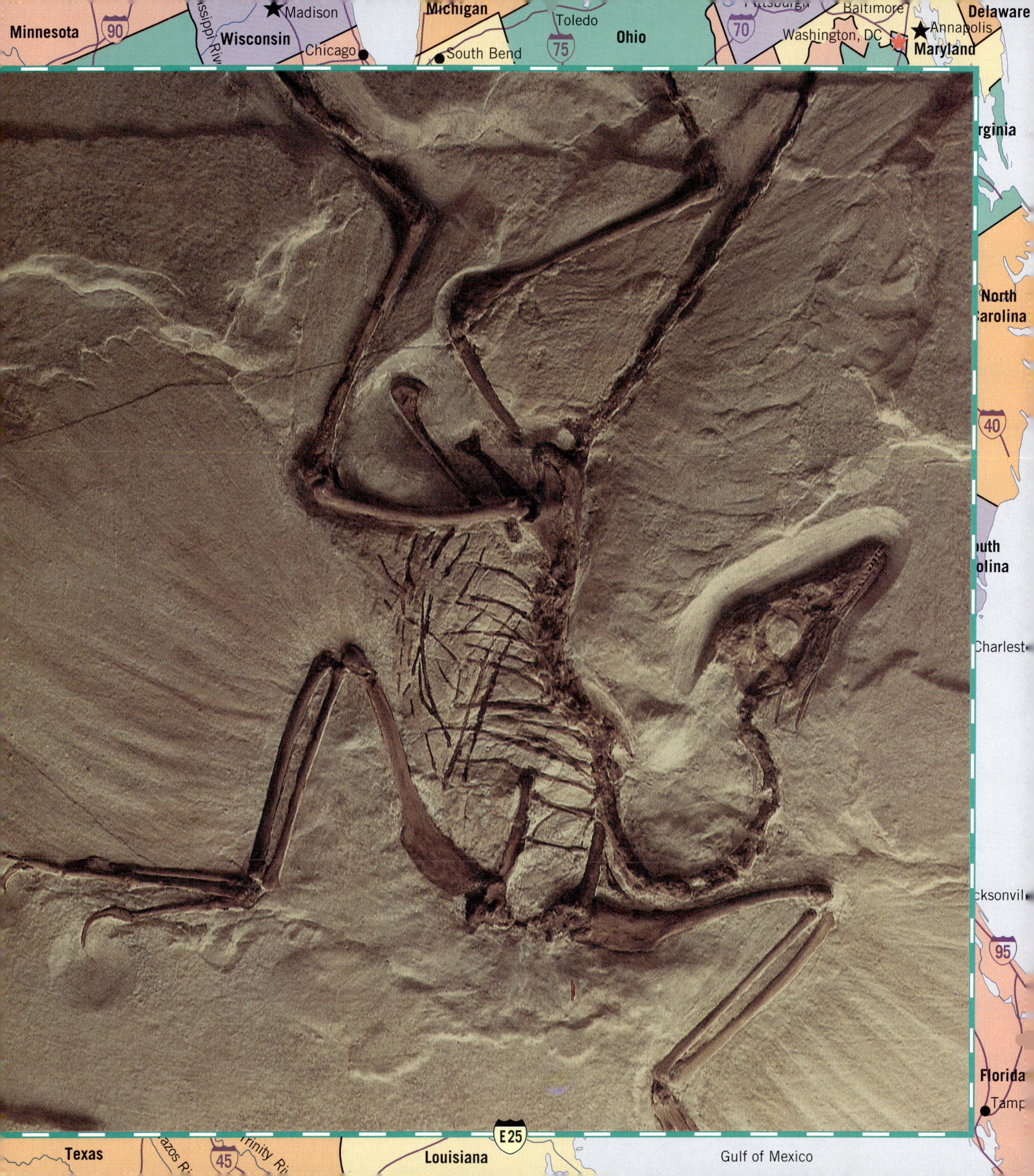
Minnesota
90
Wisconsin
Madison
Chicago
Michigan
South Bend
Toledo
75
Ohio
70
Baltimore
Washington, DC
Annapolis
Delaware
Maryland
North Carolina
40
Charlest
95
Florida
Tamp
Texas
45
Louisiana
E25
Gulf of Mexico

What are fossils?

What was the earth like in the past? Some clues to the earth's past can be found in rocks. Certain rocks contain fossils. **Fossils** are preserved evidence of ancient living things. They usually form when organisms die and are covered by sediments. Fossils tell us about plants and animals that once lived on the earth. Scientists who study the prehistoric life of plants and animals are paleontologists (pā´lē ən täl´ə jists).

The soft parts of living things, such as leaves, skin, and muscles, decay quickly. Fossils usually are the remains of the hard parts of an organism, such as wood, shells, bones, and teeth.

Because not all parts of animals and plants become preserved as fossils, paleontologists often must piece together a few parts of an organism. In order to rebuild an ancient plant or animal, they use what they know about similar organisms from the past. They also use their knowledge of plants and animals that live on the earth today.

▲ Some fossils are the actual remains of a plant or animal. Animals like this fragile insect have been found preserved in hardened tree sap, called amber. Woolly mammoths, which were as large as modern adult elephants, have been discovered frozen in ice.

Sometimes after an organism is buried, water rich in minerals dissolves the original organic matter. When this original material is preserved, the plant or animal is petrified (pe´tri fīd´), or turned to stone. This fossil is petrified wood. ▶

▲ When an organism is buried and squeezed between layers of sediments, the fluids are removed from the organism. A thin film of carbon remains and an imprint is left.

Be a Scientist

HANDS-ON ACTIVITY

Can you make a fossil?

1. ACTIVITY JOURNAL Choose an object to make your own mold and cast fossils. Coat your object with a thin film of petroleum jelly. Gently push the object into some modeling clay. Carefully remove the object. What kind of fossil did you make?
2. Now coat the impression you made with petroleum jelly. Fill the impression with plaster of Paris.
3. When the plaster is dry, remove it from the impression. What kind of fossil did you make? Exchange fossils with a classmate and try to write descriptions of the original objects. What information could you infer from this fossil? What information could you not infer?

◀ A fossilized mold forms if buried organic material dissolves to leave an empty space that is the shape of the original organism or its parts. If this space becomes filled with minerals or sediments, then a fossil cast forms. A cast takes the shape of the original organism or its parts.

How do scientists determine the age of rocks?

▲ Trilobites are good index fossils because they were numerous and widely distributed over the earth for a short period of time.

Suppose you get a newspaper delivered to your home each day. After the newspaper is read, you put it into a box. If you do this after you read each paper every day, the oldest newspaper will be on the bottom of the box and the most recent paper will be on the top. If the pile is not disturbed, the newspapers will remain in this order, or sequence.

Much like your stack of newspapers, scientists have found that in areas where rocks are undisturbed, the oldest rocks are on the bottom. The youngest rocks are near the top. This kind of sequencing is called relative dating. Using this method, scientists are able to determine that one rock layer is older or younger than another. Often, relative dating is used to date sedimentary rock layers.

Then, too, scientists use fossils to determine the age of rocks. Different-aged rocks contain different fossil groupings. Fossilized organisms occur in a definite order within rocks. Thus, a time period in the earth's past can be predicted by the fossils contained in its rocks.

Some fossils clearly indicate the age of a rock. These are called **index fossils.** In order to be an index fossil, three conditions must be met. First, an

SCIENCE JOURNAL

Look at some old family photos. How have you and your family changed? How are you the same? Take several photos, each taken in a different year, and mix them up. Would you be able to sort the pictures from the oldest to the most recent? What clues would you use? Write your ideas in your Science Journal. Then have a family member try to put the pictures in order.

BACK HOME

▲ Paleontologists use index fossils to date rocks. An index fossil can indicate a rock's age fairly accurately.

organism must have been abundant. Next, the organism must have existed for only a short period. Finally, the organism must have changed, or evolved, rapidly.

Trilobites (trī´lō bīts´) are animals that lived hundreds of millions of years ago. They are index fossils that have been found in a rock layer at the bottom of the Grand Canyon and in a rock layer in Wales. From this, scientists infer that both rock layers are about the same age.

What is another way that scientists determine the ages of rocks?

Think about the Back Home activity on page E28. Unless you knew when each photograph was taken, you could probably say only that one was newer or older than another. In the same way, when scientists use relative dating methods, they can say only that one rock layer is younger or older than another.

Imagine that your camera could record the date and time of day that a photo was taken. You could use this information to put the pictures in order according to the exact time each was taken. In a similar way, the actual ages of some rocks can be determined by a method called radiometric dating.

Scientists use a form of radiometric dating called carbon-14 dating to determine the age of once-living organisms. Also, scientists are able to date rocks that have fossils in them because fossils were once living. In this process, the amounts of two elements are measured. One of these elements is a radioactive element that changes at a constant rate into another element. The other element that is measured is the one that the radioac-

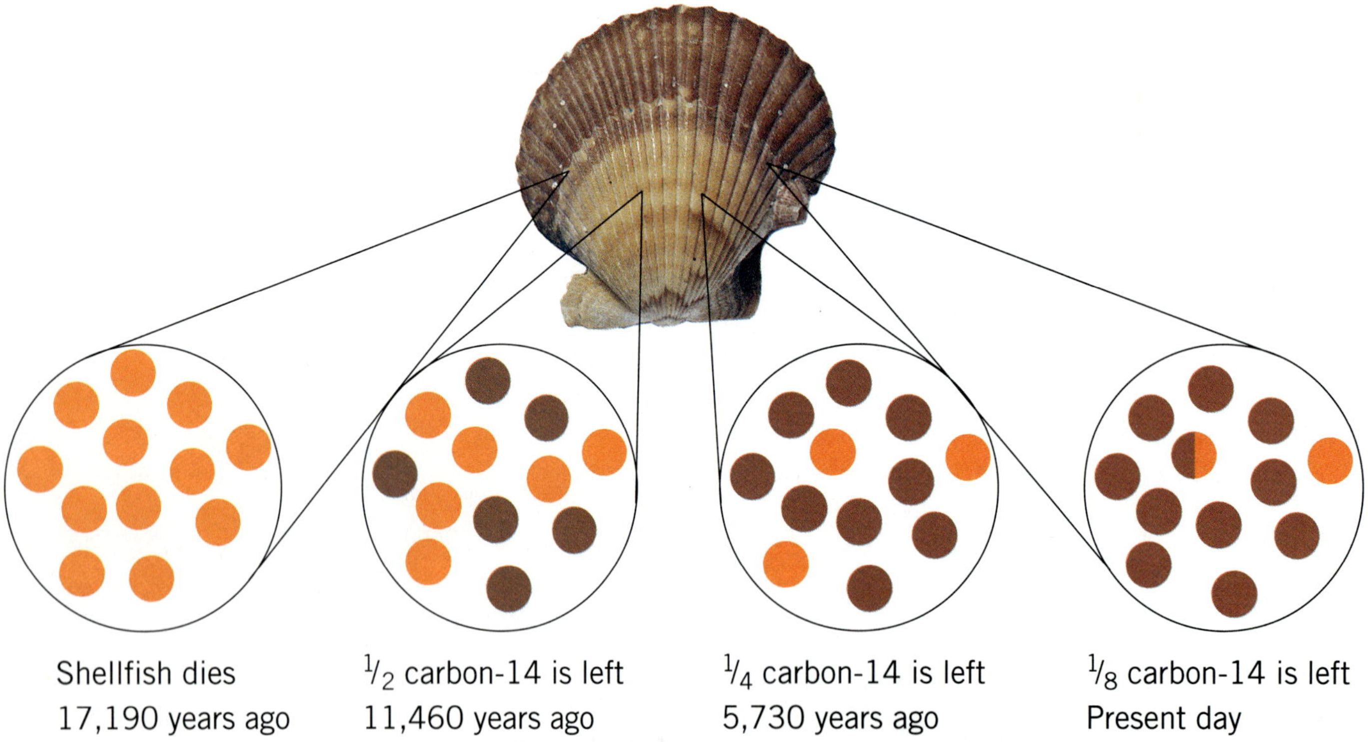

HISTORY

The Age of the Earth

The San Andreas fault system is between 15 and 20 million years old. This is considered a very young feature on our planet! Most scientists agree that our planet is about 4.6 billion years old. What was the earth like 4.6 billion years ago? What is your theory on how it formed?

Most scientists believe that the universe formed about 15 billion years ago. The big-bang theory is about an explosion that caused matter to fly outward from a central point. A swirling cloud of hot gases and dust slowly cooled over billions of years to form our solar system. Gravity caused much of the matter to be pulled toward the center of the cloud. This matter eventually became our sun. Other particles collected to form the planets. Radiometric dating of meteorites, materials from the moon, and certain earth rocks suggests that the earth is about 4.6 billion years old.

tive element changes into. By comparing the amounts of each element, a fossil's age can be determined.

Organisms collect carbon-14 during their lives. When a plant or animal dies, no more carbon-14 enters the organism and the remaining carbon-14 in the organism continues to decay. If the amount of carbon-14 is compared to the amount of decay product, scientists can determine when the organism died.

The decay rate of radioactive elements, like carbon, never changes. Carbon-14 decays at a predictable rate. Thus, scientists can measure the amount of carbon-14 in a once-living organism and use that measurement to calculate its age.

In the oldest rocks that have fossil remains, most of the radioactive elements have changed to other elements.

◀ Radioactive elements decay, or change into new elements, at a constant rate. These elements can be used to determine the approximate ages of certain fossils.

How are you doing?

1. What are some ways organisms can be preserved as fossils?
2. Name three ways the earth's rocks can be dated.
3. **Think** How is the radioactive element carbon-14 used to determine the age of fossils? Explain.
4. **Think** Worms have no hard parts. Yet, scientists know that they've been on the earth for millions of years. How might a scientist find out about ancient worms?

What is geologic time?

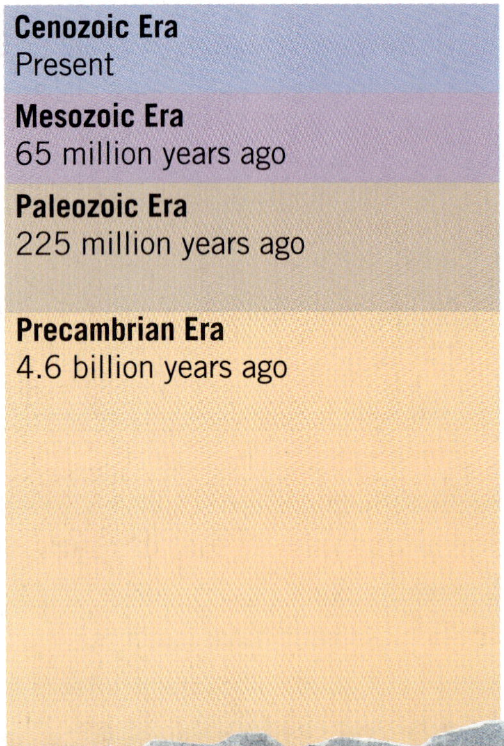

The earth's history is very long. Scientists have determined that the earth is about 4.6 billion years old. This is a great amount of time that is hard to imagine. If this time could be squeezed into one year, humans would be on the earth for less than a blink of your eye.

Scientists use a **geologic time scale** to show the earth's history and its life. The earth's history can be divided into four major segments that are called eras. Eras are defined by the different plants and animals that lived during that time. The close of each era is marked by many extinctions of plants and animals. Eras are not of equal lengths of time.

Precambrian Era
4.6 billion years before present

Precambrian Era

The Precambrian (prē kam´brē ən) Era is the longest unit of geologic time. It lasted for almost 4 billion years. Mountains formed and eroded away. Glaciers covered much of the land at times. Little is known about this era because few fossils have been found. After the earth began to take form, it was hundreds of millions of years before the first life evolved. About 3,500 million years ago the first cells appeared. Millions of years later fungi and algae evolved. Then organisms such as jellyfish and sponges appeared.

Paleozoic Era

During the Paleozoic (pā´lēō zō´ik) Era, the earth's land formed a supercontinent called Pangaea. Toward the end of the era, the Appalachian Mountains began to form. The climate was warm and the landscape barren. Many organisms lived in the warm, shallow seas that covered much of the planet. Sea animals with shells and external skeletons thrived. Many invertebrates, such as trilobites, became extinct. Plants and animals developed adaptations that allowed them to live on land.

Paleozoic Era
600 to 225 million years before present

YOU CAN HELP

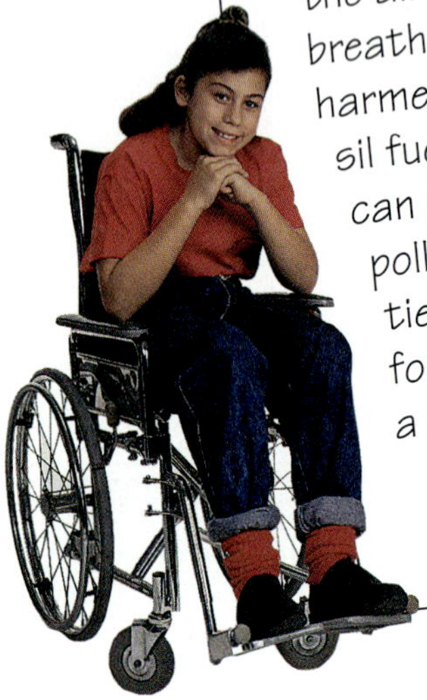

Burning fossil fuels pollutes the air you and other animals breathe. Plants, too, are harmed by pollution from fossil fuels. You and your family can help cut down on air pollution by reducing activities that involve burning fossil fuels, such as driving a car.

Mesozoic Era

The Mesozoic (mes´ō zō´ik) Era is marked by Pangaea breaking into separate continents and the Rocky Mountains forming. The climate was generally warm and sea levels rose. Dinosaurs roamed the earth for much of the era. For reasons still not known, they became extinct, along with other animals and plants. During this era fish, reptiles, and large mollusks lived in the seas. One mollusk, the ammonite, resembled some of today's snails. Small mammals, birds, snakes, and flowering plants appeared on land.

Mesozoic Era
225 to 65 million years before present

HISTORY

Coal—One Source of Energy

Coal is the remains of plants that lived long ago. When plants died, they were attacked by bacteria that caused the plants to decay. This decayed matter was covered with sediments. Heat and pressure caused certain elements to escape, leaving behind carbon. Over millions of years, the carbon accumulated to form coal.

The living plants gathered and stored energy from the sun. When coal is burned, this stored energy is released. Explain why coal is a fossil fuel.

Cenozoic Era

During the Cenozoic (sē´nə zō´ik) Era the landmasses continued to separate and moved to present-day positions. The Himalayas rose and ice built up on Antarctica. Mountain building took place over the world as slabs of the earth's crust collided. Movement along the San Andreas fault began. Some animals, such as the woolly mammoth, became extinct. Insects and flowering plants continued to be abundant. During this era, the first humans appeared.

Cenozoic Era
65 million years ago to present

First primates | Ice Age glaciers melted | Landmasses reach present position | First humans

How are you doing?

1. On what are the divisions of the geologic time scale based?
2. Briefly describe some of the events that happened during the Paleozoic and Mesozoic eras.
3. **Think** Compare and contrast the dominant life forms in each era.
4. **Think** Describe a general pattern, or trend, in the kinds of life that lived on the earth over geologic time.

Earth Legends

Earthquakes and other natural occurences have been happening for millions of years. Yet, scientists have understood what causes earthquakes for only about 30 years.

Ancient peoples all over the world have explanations about these natural occurences and how they have affected their way of life. These explanations, passed on by word of mouth, are called legends.

Many American Indian legends tell about the earth and its inhabitants. These stories do not try to explain facts scientifically. Instead, they explain certain beliefs.

One story tells how the Navajos came to be. The legend says that the Navajos rose from the center of the earth through a hollow reed. The first Navajo home, or hogan, was built on this spot. The legend divides the earth into four sections. Each section has a sacred mountain and a person who guards it. Today, most Navajos live in the sacred homeland called Dinétah in Colorado and New Mexico. This area is bordered by four mountains: Blanca Peak, Francisco Peak, Mount Taylor, and Hesperus Mountain.

Another legend of the Navajo people explains the relationship between the earth and the sky. The photograph is a sandpainting of Mother Earth and Father Sky, the two halves of Navajo creation. Plants grow from Mother Earth. The stars belong to Father Sky.

Data Collection and Analysis

How much is a billion?

The earth is about 4.6 billion years old. This is such a big number that it's hard to imagine. In this activity, determine the number of containers needed to hold one billion objects.

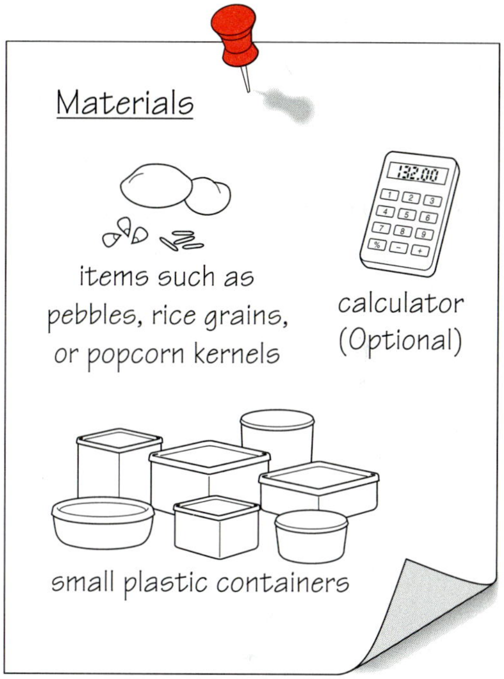

Observe and Collect Data

1. Work in groups. Select an object. Count the number of items in a container. Then estimate how many containers it will take to hold 1 billion objects. Complete the table below in your Activity Journal.
2. Add the results from at least three other groups to your table.

Draw Conclusions

1. How did your estimate of the number of containers compare with the actual number that it took? Why do you think you estimated the way you did?
2. Compare your description of one billion with those of your classmates. What do the descriptions have in common? How are they different?
3. How does your new understanding of a billion affect how you now think about the age of the earth?

Counting to a Billion

A	B	C
Number of objects in a container	Number of containers for 1 million 1,000,000/A =	Number of containers for 1 billion B x 1000 =

Looking Back

Words and Concepts

Match the description in Column A with the correct term in Column B.

Column A

1. Method used by scientists to determine the exact age of a rock
2. An impression in the shape of a once-living organism
3. The longest unit of geologic time
4. Organisms that no longer live on the earth
5. Mammals appeared in this era
6. Plants and animals first inhabited land in this era

Column B

a. Mesozoic Era
b. Radiometric dating
c. Extinct life
d. Precambrian Era
e. Fossil mold
f. Paleozoic Era

Applied Thinking Skills

Answer the following questions. You can use words, drawings, and diagrams in your answers.

7. Describe the organisms that lived during the early part of the Paleozoic Era. Contrast organisms with those that lived at the end of the era.
8. Explain some conditions that are necessary for fossil formation.
9. **Your World** Describe two ways you could create fossils that could provide clues about you for scientists in the future.

Some whale bone fossils are too big and heavy to hold. This is a small vertebra.

Show What You Know

Can you make a geologic clock?

Observe and Collect Data

1. Make a circle that is divided into 24 equal segments to represent a 24-hour day. This can be approximated by dividing the circle into thirds and then halving each section three times.
2. Use the data in the table below to plot the earth's history on the 24-hour graph. Color each section.
3. Make a key that explains what each color represents.
4. Make a 24-hour circle graph that shows how you might spend a day. Include a color key.

Draw Conclusions

1. Study your clock of the earth's history. What can you say about the amount of time that life has been present on the earth?
2. Compare your clock with the geologic clock. Which activity or activities can be compared to the Precambrian Era?
3. Which activity do you spend the least amount of time doing? Which geologic era is this activity "equivalent" to?

Process Skills
Measuring, Making models, Interpreting data

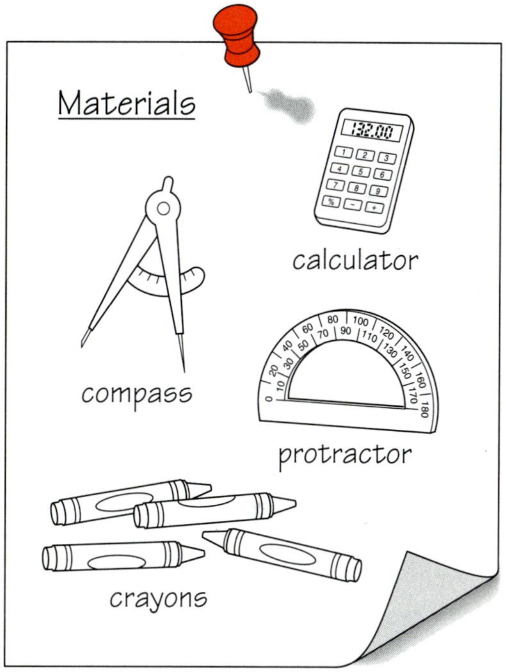

Unit of geologic time	Actual time in years	Time in 24-hour model
Precambrian Era	4.03 billion	20 hours, 52 minutes
Paleozoic Era	375 million	1 hour, 58 minutes
Mesozoic Era	160 million	48 minutes
Cenozoic Era	65 million	22 minutes

Chapter 3

The Earth's Plates

▲ Earth scientists investigating a fissure or ground rupture, caused by the 1989 Loma Prieta earthquake.

▲ A road and fence were displaced by the 1906 San Francisco earthquake.

Slabs made of the earth's crust and rigid upper mantle ride on the hot, semisolid part of the mantle, which has the consistency of modeling clay. As these rigid slabs move slowly across the earth's surface, mountains form. Ocean basins open and close. These movements that are taking place today also took place millions and billions of years ago. It wasn't until the 1960s that geologists were able to make these conclusions.

Throughout history, scientists have made many hypotheses, or guesses, about how our planet formed and how and why it constantly changes. Many of these hypotheses were changed as more data were collected. Our current explanation is a model called plate tectonics. The theory of **plate tectonics** states that the earth's crust and upper mantle are broken into huge slabs. These slabs, or **plates**, are joined much like the pieces of a jigsaw puzzle. There are up to 12 major plates in our earth's outer rock shell.

It is not known exactly why these plates are in constant motion and how they move slowly across the earth's surface. Scientists have speculated that the earth's internal heat causes convection currents in the semisolid mantle. The convection currents under the floating plates cause the plates to move.

SCIENCE JOURNAL The students in the photograph are standing along the San Andreas fault. This fault separates two of the earth's plates. Think about what you have just read. Make a hypothesis about why earthquakes happen along the San Andreas fault. Write your hypothesis in your Science Journal.

Matching ground surface features to our San Andreas fault map

Explore Activity

Can you model the earth's plates?

Process Skills
Observing, Communicating, Defining operationally

Observe and Collect Data

1. Pour the dirt into the container.
2. Add enough water to make a thick, soupy paste. Stir the mixture with the spoon until it is smooth.
3. Carefully pour the mixture into the cookie sheet. Use the spoon to spread the mixture evenly over the whole cookie sheet.

4. Put the cookie sheet in the sun or a warm place where it can dry. Choose a location where the sheet will not be disturbed.

5. ACTIVITY JOURNAL After the mud has dried, study the slab to see if you can determine lines or zones of weakness. **Predict** where you think the mud slab might crack. Record your observations in your Activity Journal. Make a sketch to support your prediction. To crack the mud slab, get a partner to help you to gently twist the corners of the sheet in opposite directions.

Share Your Results

Compare and contrast your "mud puzzle" with those of at least two other pairs of students. How did your prediction of how the slab might crack compare with how the slab actually did crack? Write your observations in your Activity Journal.

Draw Conclusions

1. How is your model like the earth's tectonic plates?
2. What kinds of things about the earth's plates can't be shown with your model?

Apply What You Know

Carefully, remove all the pieces of your puzzle from the cookie sheet. Work with your partner to try to put it back together. How might this activity be like one in which scientists try to reconstruct ancient landmasses?

What evidence supports plate tectonics?

The four global maps show how the drifting continents may have moved from 500 million years ago to the present time. ▶

In 1912, a German scientist named Alfred Wegener proposed that landmasses had drifted across the earth to their present positions. This hypothesis was called **continental drift**. Wegener based his hypothesis on several pieces of evidence. He collected evidence from the rocks, fossils, and climates of different continents. His evidence supported his hypothesis that continents had once been joined together. He noted that the coast of eastern South America seemed to fit like a puzzle piece into the western coast of Africa. He also observed that many of the rock formations on the two continents were similar.

Another line of evidence came from fossils. Similar fossils were found in similar rocks on different continents. Also, fossils of certain organisms seemed out of place. For example, fossils of a plant called *Glossopteris* (gläs äp´tər əs) have been found on all the continents in the Southern Hemisphere. *Glossopteris* lived in temperate, humid regions. How could this plant have survived on present-day Antarctica?

Even though Wegener's argument was supported by numerous observations, most scientists rejected his hypothesis of continental drift. Why? Wegener could not explain *how* such enormous masses of land could

Be a Scientist

HANDS-ON ACTIVITY

Can you model convection currents?

1. A convection current is movement in a fluid when hot fluid rises and cold fluid sinks. These currents are thought to drive the movements of the earth's plates. Use a clear, heat-resistant container to observe similar currents. Fill your container $\frac{3}{4}$ full of water.
2. Add $\frac{1}{2}$ cup of rice or popcorn kernels to the water. Carefully bring the water to a slow boil. Observe the movements of the rice or popcorn.
3. ACTIVITY JOURNAL Draw a picture of your observations in your Activity Journal. How might this movement be like the movement that drives the earth's plates?

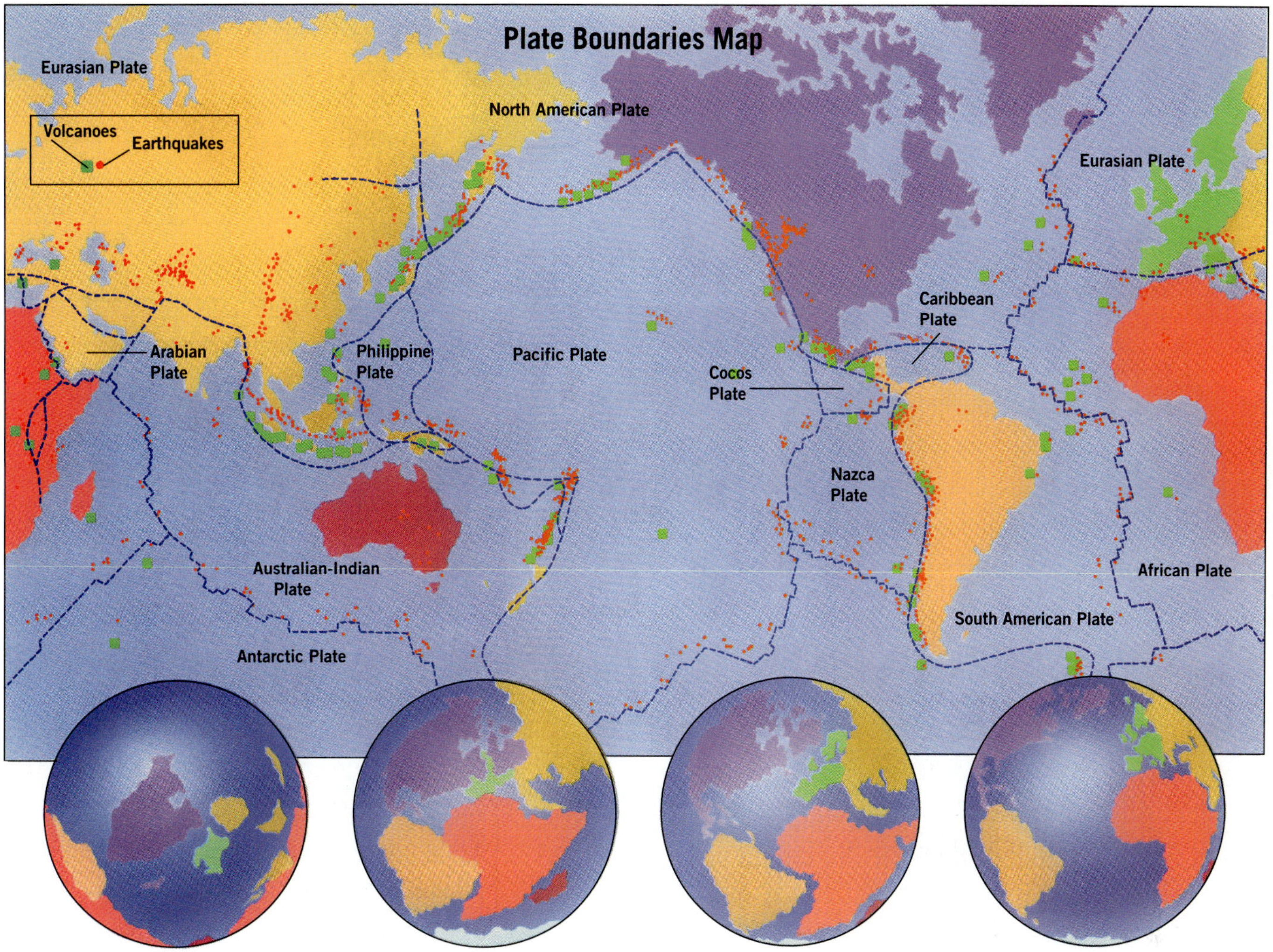

500 million years ago | 250 million years ago | 100 million years ago | Present

move around. Wegener thought that the continents moved through the mantle like a plow moves through soil.

It wasn't until the early 1960s, when scientists were able to map the ocean bottoms, that evidence was gathered to support continental drift. Maps of the ocean bottom revealed that the basins were very young features. The maps also showed that near the middle of the Atlantic and Indian oceans there is a long narrow mid-ocean ridge. One ridge system is called the Mid-Atlantic Ridge. Red-hot lava from the mantle flows from these ridges and adds new ocean floor material to the earth. Rocks closest to the ridge are younger than rocks farther from the ridge. The scientists realized that the ocean floors are spreading apart. This process of making new ocean crust is called **sea-floor spreading**, and it occurs along certain plate boundaries.

How do plates move?

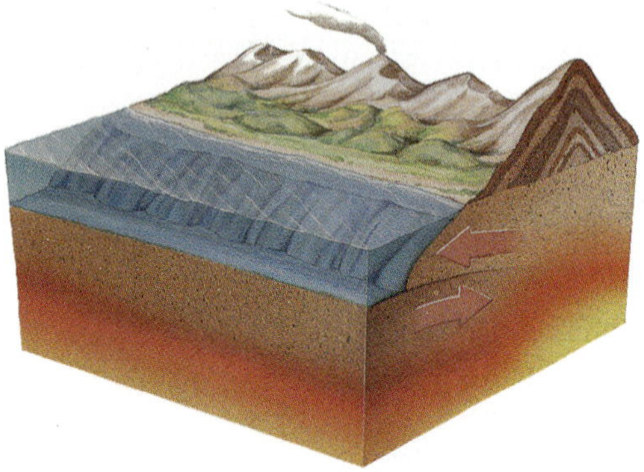

▲ Convergent boundary

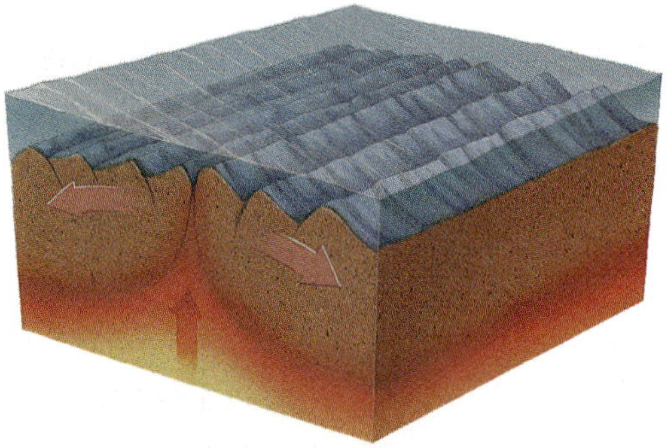

▲ Divergent boundary

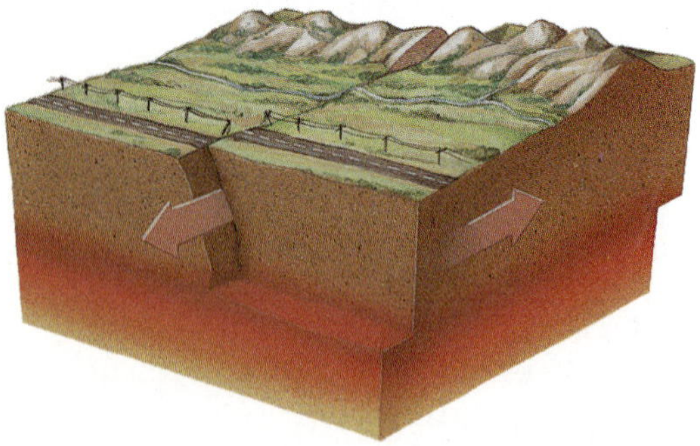

▲ Transform-fault boundary

Plates come into contact with one another at three types of boundaries. In some places, plates collide. Sometimes they separate. And sometimes plates move sideways past each other.

Places where two plates collide or come together are called **convergent boundaries.** What do you think might happen when two enormous plates of rock push against each other? Sometimes, the plates buckle and

DILEMMA

Burying Hazardous Wastes

Some people have suggested burying containers of radioactive waste at certain convergent boundaries. Their reasoning is that this dangerous material, which can cause problems if buried near the surface, will be taken deep into the earth.

Think About It Do you think this is a good idea? Why or why not? Should the containers be buried at boundaries that are colliding slowly or quickly? Why? Organize a class debate on this topic.

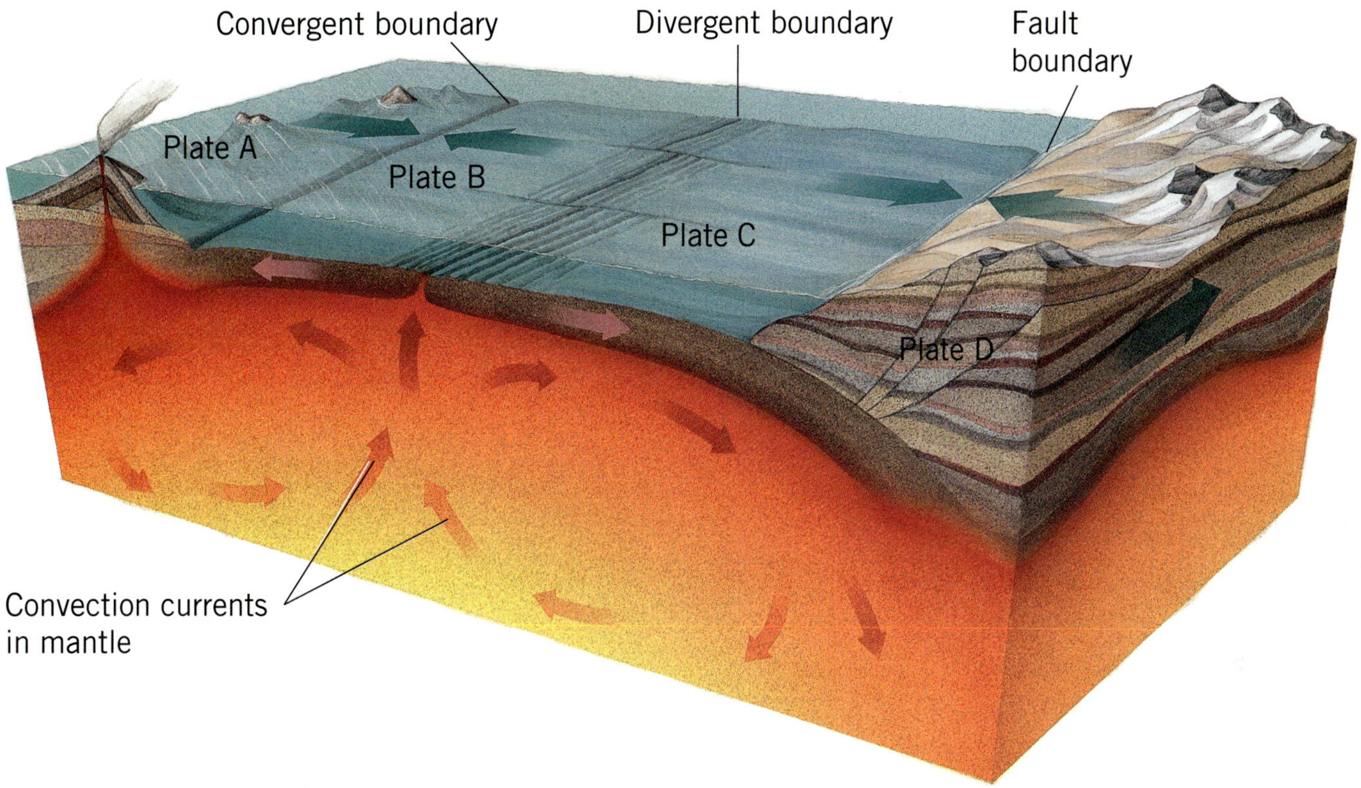

rise to form mountains. In other cases, one plate slides beneath the other. As the lower plate sinks into the mantle, it melts. The magma that forms from this melting plate may slowly rise to produce volcanoes.

Plates move apart at **divergent boundaries.** As plates separate, magma rises to fill the gap. When the magma hardens, new ocean crust is formed. Divergent boundaries most often occur on the ocean floor along mid-ocean ridges.

Transform faults are the third type of plate boundary. At a **transform-fault boundary**, plates move horizontally past each other. The plates make contact with each other at a fault. Earthquakes are very common along these boundaries. The San Andreas fault is a transform-fault boundary.

▲ The theory of plate tectonics states that the earth's crust and upper mantle are broken into large slabs called plates. Convection currents in the mantle cause these plates to move slowly across the earth's surface. Some plates move fewer than 1.5 centimeters per year. Other plates move between 10 and 20 centimeters yearly, or about as fast as your fingernails grow.

How are you doing?

1. What is the theory of plate tectonics?
2. What is sea-floor spreading?
3. Think Compare and contrast convergent and divergent boundaries.
4. Think If continental landmasses were once joined, why don't they fit together perfectly today? How might these landmasses look 50 million years from now?

What are earthquakes?

An earthquake sends seismic waves through the earth. The point where the earthquake starts is called the **focus.** Although they can be as deep as 700 km, the focuses of most earthquakes are shallow, usually less than 100 km deep. The point on the earth's surface directly above the focus is called the **epicenter** (ep´i sent ər). Epicenters are usually in narrow zones called belts, where mountain building and volcanic activity are present. ▼

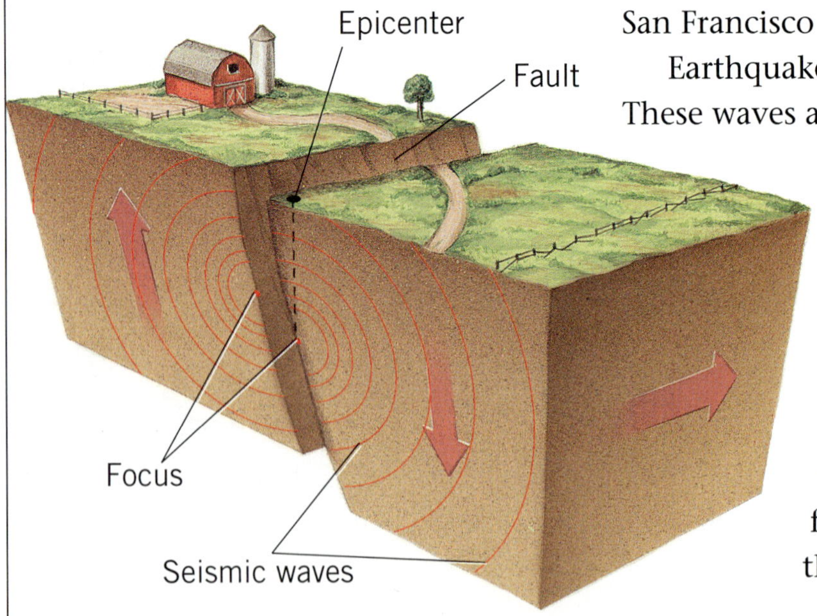

An earthquake is a trembling, a vibration, or motion of the earth. Earthquakes happen when the ground shakes suddenly and rapidly as energy that has been slowly building up in the earth's crust is released in the crust or upper mantle. Most earthquakes happen because rocks move past each other along faults. More than 900,000 earthquakes occur each year. Thousands of them occur in California, with many due to movement along the San Andreas fault. Most earthquakes aren't felt by people. Others do enormous amounts of damage.

One of the most damaging earthquakes on the San Andreas fault occurred in 1906. It struck the area around San Francisco. Scientists estimate that the San Francisco earthquake released 60 times more energy than the Loma Prieta earthquake of 1989. Fires, some of which started from broken gas lines, raged for days after the San Francisco earthquake.

Earthquakes send out energy waves in all directions. These waves are called seismic waves. Seismic waves that travel through the earth's interior are called body waves. Seismic waves that move through the earth's crust are called surface waves.

There are two kinds of body waves, P-(Primary) waves and S-(Secondary) waves. P-waves always travel faster than S-waves. Body waves help us locate the focus of an earthquake. P-waves travel through molten and solid rocks. They cause

Be a Scientist

How do earthquake waves travel?

1. Wear your safety goggles throughout this activity. Work with two other people. Two people in your group need to hold the ends of a coiled spring toy and stretch it to about 2 meters. While the spring is stretched, the third person squeezes together about 20 of the coils, then releases them. Switch roles so that each person can observe what happens.
2. ACTIVITY JOURNAL Draw your observations in your Activity Journal. You may want to make notes.
3. Next, two people in your group hold the ends of the spring. One of them makes a quick flip of the wrist to the right to set the spring in motion. Switch roles so each person can observe what happens. Draw a picture of your observations.
4. Finally, two people hold the ends of the spring. One of them moves the spring up and down while the other person moves the spring sideways. Switch roles and record your observations.

the rock particles to be pushed together and pulled apart, which causes the ground to stretch and then compress. S-waves also travel through rocks. They cause rock particles to move at right angles to the wave movement, which causes the ground to vibrate sideways. S-waves do not travel through the outer core.

There are two kinds of surface waves. One kind of surface wave travels sideways. They cause the ground to shake from side to side, much the way a snake moves. The other surface waves have up-and-down motion and can open and close cracks in the earth. The surface waves are usually responsible for shaking the ground.

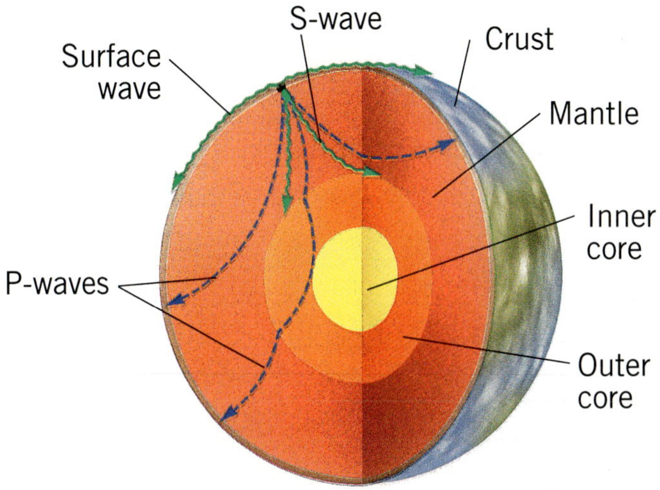

▲ The study of earthquake waves allowed scientists to divide our planet into three major layers—the crust, the mantle, and the core. How do you think scientists found out that the outer core was liquid?

How are earthquakes detected?

Earthquakes have been happening on the earth since it formed 4.6 billion years ago. These events are more common in some places than others. Look at the map on page E45. Where do most earthquakes occur? Why do you think earthquakes happen where they do?

Many earthquakes, such as those that occur along the San Andreas fault, are recorded with an instrument called a seismograph (sīz´mə graf´). A seismograph records the direction, intensity, and duration of earthquakes. One type of seismograph has a mass, which is a quanity of matter, that hangs from a support. The support is anchored in the ground. When an earthquake occurs, the mass vibrates, and movement is recorded as a zigzag line on a rotating drum.

The information recorded by a seismograph is called a seismogram. P-waves are the

Be a Scientist

HANDS-ON ACTIVITY

Can you make a seismograph?

1. Stack several books in a pile on a cart with wheels. Anchor a ruler between the top two books. Now attach a washer and clay to a pen with rubber bands as shown in the photograph.
2. ACTIVITY JOURNAL Put a sheet of paper under the pen. Make sure the pen tip just touches the paper. Have your partner hold the books in place while you gently shake the cart to produce an "earthquake." What do you see on the paper?
3. Take turns producing "earthquakes." Describe how different forces produce different seismograms.

Geophysicist

Rufus Catchings is a geophysicist who conducts scientific investigations related to earthquakes, volcanoes, mineral exploration, and nuclear safety. Some geophysicists conduct studies on the temperature of rocks, electrical energy in rocks, magnetism of various rocks, and the stress and strain in rocks. This information is applied to fields of study such as mineral and oil exploration, volcano research, earthquake research, tectonic studies, and environmental studies.

"Much of my research is on understanding the San Andreas fault and other faults that pose a threat to public safety. I conduct experiments on how seismic waves travel through the earth. I also study the composition of the earth and what it is like at great depths.

"I studied mathematics, physics, electrical engineering, and earth science in college and later earned a doctorate degree. I now do research for the United States Geological Survey.

"I like my job because the type of research that I do can actually save lives. One of the best things about my job is that the whole earth is my laboratory."

fastest seismic waves, so they arrive first and are recorded first. S-waves, which travel about half as fast as P-waves, arrive next. The last seismic waves to arrive and be recorded are the surface waves.

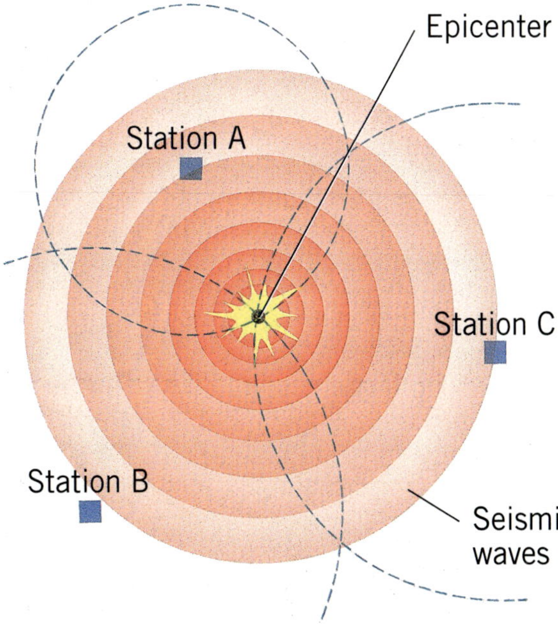

Arrival times recorded on seismographs give the distance of the earthquake from three or more recording stations. Circles are drawn to represent the distance from each station to the focus. The point where the circles intersect is the epicenter of the earthquake. ▶

How are earthquakes measured?

Two scales measure earthquakes. Both scales use numbers to describe how strong earthquakes are.

The Mercalli scale was developed in 1902 by Giuseppe Mercalli, an Italian geologist. This scale uses Roman numerals from I to XII to describe the intensity of the physical effects of an earthquake. A gentle earthquake not felt by people is rated I. Earthquakes that produce heavy damage are rated IX. If there is total destruction, the earthquake is rated XI or XII, the highest value on the scale.

The Richter scale was developed in 1935 by Charles Richter, an American physicist. This scale ranks earthquakes with Arabic numbers according to the amount of energy released. The Richter scale is very accurate because it uses scientific instruments to measure ground motion.

SCIENCE JOURNAL

Most earthquakes occur around the Pacific Ocean. But earthquakes can happen anywhere in the world. Consider what you've learned about earthquake damage. With a family member, identify and list potential earthquake hazards in your home. If possible, make changes to reduce potential hazards. Compare your list to your classmates' lists.

BACK HOME

▲ Unreinforced brick walls can collapse during strong earthquakes.

Some wood-frame structures may not collapse if they are well built and bolted to their foundations.

Richter Scale

< 3.5	Recorded but generally not felt
3.5–5.4	Only minor damage detected
5.5–6.0	Slight damage to structures
6.1–6.9	Can be destructive in populated areas
7.0–7.9	Major earthquakes that inflict serious damage
≥ 8.0	Great earthquakes that produce total destruction to nearby communities

The vibrations produced by an earthquake can cause freeway overpasses to collapse.

SIDE TRIP

The New Madrid Fault

Most earthquakes occur along plate boundaries. One of the most intense earthquakes in the United States, however, occurred far from any plate boundary. The New Madrid fault is a system of active faults buried thousands of meters below sand and mud in Illinois, Missouri, Kentucky, Tennessee, and Arkansas. In 1811, movement along the New Madrid fault zone caused more than 2,000 shock waves. Five of these tremors would have measured 8.0 or greater on the Richter scale. Scientists predict that the next powerful earthquake along this fault system will be between the years 2000 and 2050.

How are you doing?

1. How does a seismograph work?
2. What is the Richter scale?
3. **Think** Compare and contrast seismic surface waves and seismic body waves.
4. **Think** What is the value of having two scales to measure earthquakes? How do they give you different information?

What is a volcano?

A **volcano** is a mountain that forms when lava, ashes, rocks, and melted rock material piles up and hardens. Volcanoes are found on landmasses and on ocean floors. Volcanoes, like earthquakes, are common along plate boundaries because where plates collide or

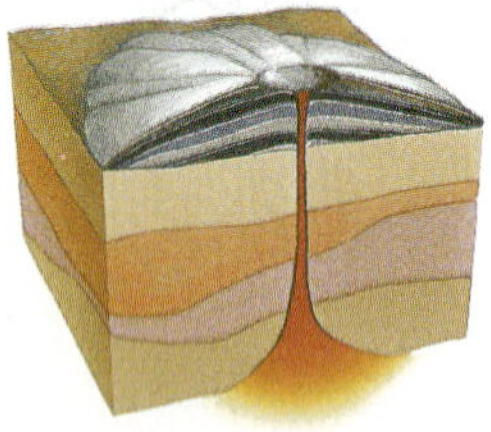

Shield volcanoes

are gently sloped volcanic mountains. They usually erupt quietly and without much force. **Shield volcanoes** are made mostly of the igneous rock basalt, which results from lava flows. The Hawaiian Islands are made of five shield volcanoes that formed as the Pacific plate moved over a hot spot in the mantle. Mauna Loa on the island of Hawaii is the largest volcano on the earth.

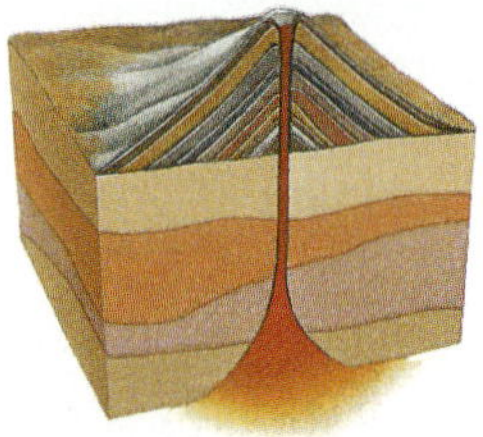

Cinder cones

are volcanoes with steep sides. They erupt with explosive force, throwing out volcanic ash and cinders, which are lava fragments. Krakatau, in Indonesia, has many small **cinder-cone** volcanoes. In 1883, it exploded and most of the mountain was blown away! The noise from the eruption could be heard in Australia. The ash was so thick it blocked the sun's light as far as 150 kilometers away.

pull apart, a vast amount of energy is released. This energy creates heat that causes the parts of the plates to melt and form magma. This magma rises toward the earth's surface to form volcanoes.

Some volcanoes form when plates drift over hot spots in the mantle. The heat from the hot spots causes the plate above to melt. As the plate continues to move, the magma rises and forms volcanoes.

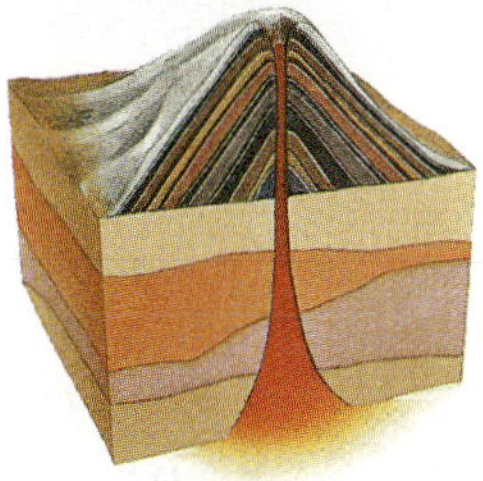

Composite cones are volcanoes made of alternating layers of volcanic rock fragments, lava, and ash. The volcanic rock and ash are ejected with great force. The lava escapes during quiet eruptions. A well-known **composite cone** is Mount Vesuvius in Italy. The composite cone shown in the photograph is Mount Shishaldin in Alaska. It is the highest peak in the Aleutian mountain range. It is nearly 3,000 meters high.

Be a Scientist

Can you model a volcano?

1. Take a sheet of blank paper and roll it into a cone. Use a piece of tape to hold the cone together. Gently fold the cone so that it lies flat.
2. On one side of your model, use colored pencils to show what the outside of a volcano might look like. On the other side of your model, show what the inside of your volcano might look like.
3. 

In your Activity Journal, write the type of volcano you made and its characteristics. Show your volcano to a classmate and see if he or she can identify it.

What is Mount St. Helens?

Mount St. Helens is a composite volcano in Washington state. This mountain is a part of the Cascade Range, a chain of volcanoes that formed when the Pacific plate collided with the North American plate millions of years ago. For more than 100 years, scientists had thought that the volcano was inactive. But on May 18, 1980, the volcano spewed tons of volcanic debris into the air. What caused this eruption? How did it affect the mountain and nearby areas? Has the area around this volcano recovered from the blast?

Imagine how a shaken soda pop explodes out of its can when it is opened. Mount St. Helens also erupted as a violent explosion. This happened because the lava was thick and the water in the lava was superheated, and because of the mixture of chemicals in the lava.

▲ Earthquakes and superheated steam in lava may have caused a bulge to form on the north slope of the volcano.

▲ Just after 8:00 a.m. on May 18, 1980, Mount St. Helens erupted. This explosion blew away the upper 550 meters of the mountain.

▲ For days after the explosion, ash fell over the region. In some places, the ash was nearly 2 meters thick.

◀ Within one year, plants such as fireweed and avalanche lilies started to grow in the volcanic ash around the mountain. Over the next decade, more plants grew in the soil. Birds, deer, elk, and insects have also returned to the area.

Shortly before the explosion, an earthquake that measured 5.1 on the Richter scale sent rocks and ice tumbling down the mountain. It is not unusual for earthquake and volcanic activity to occur at the same time. During the eruption, volcanic ash and broken rocks were ejected from the mountain through an enormous hole. The temperature of the materials and gases was probably greater than 800°C. Mudflows carried rock, ash, and trees into a river. Some of this debris dammed the river and caused nearby lakes to rise tens of meters. As a result of the blast, sixty people were killed. All the plants and animals in the vicinity were destroyed by the explosion. Yet only a year later, life returned to the area around the volcano.

Amazing!

The explosion of Mount St. Helens stripped limbs from trees 25 kilometers away and caused the trees to fall like matchsticks.

How are you doing?

1. How do volcanoes form?
2. Describe what happened to Mount St. Helens on May 18, 1980.
3. **Think** Compare and contrast the three types of volcanoes.
4. **Think** Would it have been possible for animals to return to the area around Mount St. Helens before plants? Explain.

Looking Back

Words and Concepts

Complete the following statements.

1. Plates are huge slabs of the earth's _______.
2. _______ are made of volcanic rock fragments, lava, and ash.
3. Plates come together at a(n) _______ boundary.
4. Plates move apart at a(n) _______ boundary.
5. The San Andreas fault zone is a(n) _______ boundary.
6. Plates move because of _______.
7. _______ were used to support the hypothesis of the continental drift.

Applied Thinking Skills

Answer the following questions. You can use words, drawings, and diagrams in your answers.

8. How can the theory of plate tectonics explain how volcanoes form?
9. Explain how new oceanic crust forms.
10. **Your World** Look at the map of tectonic plates on page E45. How close do you live to the edge of a plate? Which plate? Why do you suppose people would want to live there? If you could live any place in the United States, where would you live? Explain your reasoning.

Show What You Know

Why do earthquakes occur along the San Andreas fault?

Observe and Collect Data

1. Use one sheet of sandpaper to sand one of the largest surfaces on each block.
2. Cut the other piece of sandpaper in half.
3. Use the thumbtacks to attach half of the sandpaper to the large, unsanded side of each block. The thumbtacks should go on the sides of the blocks.
4. ACTIVITY JOURNAL Hold a block in either hand and slide the smoothed surfaces against each other. Describe the movement. Slide the sandpapered sides against each other. Describe the movement in your Activity Journal.

Draw Conclusions

1. Which of your movements represents a day with no earthquakes along the San Andreas fault?
2. Which of your movements represents an earthquake along the fault?
3. Why do earthquakes occur?
4. How are you able to predict where earthquakes will occur? Can you predict when they will occur?

Process Skills
Inferring, Defining operationally, Making models

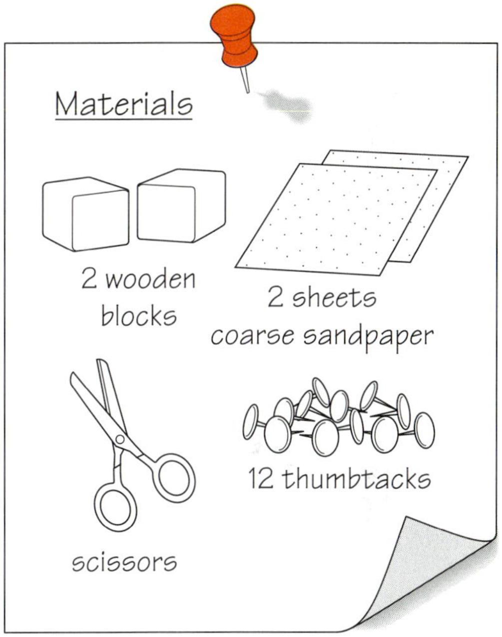

Earth Movements

Show what you have learned about the layers of the earth, the history of the earth, and plate tectonics. Work by yourself, with a partner, or in a group. Select one activity.

Model Maker Using any materials you wish, make a model of the layers of the earth. Use your model to show how plates might move, how mountains could form, or how earthquakes happen. Be sure to be as accurate as possible. Design a way to label the parts.

Journalist You are a newspaper reporter covering an earthquake. For someone who has never seen or heard of an earthquake, write a story explaining what you see and how you feel.

Songwriter Write a song about earthquakes or volcanic eruptions. Use words to describe how these events occur. Try it out on your class. How did your classmates respond to the song? Did they feel the way you thought they would?

Geologist You work for the federal government. Your job is to take people on tours of the area around the San Andreas fault. What do you tell people as they tour the area? Make a tour guidebook that can be used to follow your talk.

Science-Fiction Writer Imagine an organism that lives in the center of the earth. Write a story about how it lives. Describe its environment and what happens there. Be creative, but scientifically accurate.

Puzzle Maker Make a puzzle that tells something about the way that the continents move. You might want to include plates, earthquakes, and volcanoes. Make sure that it can be worked over and over again.

Glossary

cinder cone (sin´dər kōn) A volcano with very steep sides that erupts with explosive force. (page E54)

composite cone (kəm päz´it kōn) A volcano made of alternating layers of volcanic rock, lava, and ash. (page E55)

continental drift (kän´tə nent´'l drift) A theory that the earth's landmasses moved across the earth's surface into their present positions. (page E44)

convergent boundary (kən vər´jənt boun´də rē) A place where the earth's plates come together. (page E46)

core (kôr) The innermost layer of the earth, lying below the mantle. (page E10)

crust (krust) The outermost, thinnest, and most solid layer of the earth. (page E10)

divergent boundary (dı vər´jənt boun´də rē) A place where the earth's plates separate. (page E47)

epicenter (ep´i sent´ər) The point on the earth's surface that is directly above the focus of an earthquake. (page E48)

extinct (ek stiŋkt´) No longer existing on the earth. (page E22)

focus (fō´kəs) The place within the earth where an earthquake begins. (page E48)

fossil (fäs´əl) The preserved remains of an ancient plant or animal. (page E26)

geologic time scale (je´ə läj´ik tīm skāl) Units of time that divide the earth's history. (page E32)

index fossil (in´deks´ fäs´əl) A fossil used to determine the age of rocks. (page E28)

mantle (man´təl) The middle layer of the earth, between the crust and core. (page E10)

plate (plāt) An enormous slab of the earth's crust and rigid upper mantle. (page E40)

plate tectonics (plāt tek tän´iks) A theory that the earth's crust and rigid upper mantle move across the earth's surface due to convection currents in the partially melted mantle. (page E40)

sea-floor spreading (sē´flôr spred´iŋ) Process by which new sea floor forms as tectonic plates move apart. (page E45)

shield volcano (shēld väl kā´nō) A gently sloped mountain that erupts without much force. (page E54)

transform-fault boundary (trans´fôrm fôlt boun´də rē) A place where the earth's plates move horizontally past each other. (page E47)

volcano (väl kā´nō) A mountain that forms when melted rock material piles up and hardens. (page E54)